How to Build a

Pharmacy

Consulting

Business

YOUR RX FOR FINDING FREEDOM AND
LOVING YOUR CAREER

Blair Thielemier, PharmD

How to Build a Pharmacy Consulting Business / Blair Thielemier

—1st ed.
ISBN 978-1530354207

Table of Contents

Acknowledgements

A special thanks to my wonderful husband Chad for being my biggest supporter and source of strength, you are my heart. And to my mother Sandy who has instilled in me her passion for healthcare, work ethic and integrity, thanks for giving me the strength to tackle anything. To my father Jim for being my sounding board and sharing my unrelenting curiosity for the world, thanks for believing in me. Also to my daughter Aven who shines light and joy into all of our lives.

Also to my business coach Natalie and her BizChix community. Without their support I would have never even known about the power of using the internet to share my message. And to Jill at Ultimate WP Help for creating the most beautiful WordPress site ever at and for fixing it when I break it.

Huge thanks to the pharmacy community, who has been nothing but helpful and supportive of me. Pharmacy is one of the most underappreciated professions and I feel it is finally our time to shine in the business of healthcare. I am especially thankful to Greta for suggesting that I start my first blog and to Sandy for telling me that I should start listening to podcasts. Always listen to your friends; sometimes they will recognize your potential before you can see it!

And to my Book Launch Team for your support and encouragement, you guys have made the self-publishing process much more fun!

Introduction

Hello, I am Dr. Blair Thielemier, the Pharmapreneur Coach. I am an independent MTM consultant pharmacist living in Arkansas with my husband and daughter. I founded PharmapreneurAcademy.com in order to help other pharmacists build their clinical pharmacy consulting businesses. I am a contributing author for *Pharmacy Times* and guest host on the *Pharmacy Podcast*. More information about me can be found on my personal website *http://BTPharmacyConsulting.com*

Congratulations! You have decided to take an important first step in building your pharmacy consulting business by choosing this book.

I am excited to welcome you into the Pharmapreneur Community!

In the chapters that follow, we will focus on building and structuring your pharmacy consulting business, tips and tricks to get your first clients, identifying the many opportunities that exist for pharmacy consultants, creative options for reimbursement and using education as a marketing strategy to create relationships with your ideal clients.

This book will help you *get focused* and *get started* building your pharmacy consulting business!

I will coach you through the business-building process and help you avoid the most common barriers to getting started. By the end of this book, you will have the Rx you need for building a pharmacy consulting business that will help you find freedom and love your pharmacy career.

If you are looking for more information about how I help pharmacists seek new opportunities in pharmacy consulting and grow their businesses, I invite you to sign up for our *Pharmapreneur Community Newsletter* at BTPharmacyConsulting.com

CHAPTER 1

My Ah-Ha Moment

At six months pregnant I was let go by my employer - no insurance, no maternity, and no severance - nothing. We had only enough savings to cover my maternity leave for six weeks.

With my back against the wall and the countdown to baby ticking by, I turned to my network and pleaded for work. Thankfully, the support of the pharmacists in my community kept me from getting into real financial trouble. It was a really hard time for me. However, because of this trying experience I found my purpose: pharmacy consulting and teaching other pharmacists to become entrepreneurs. One thing is for sure, I *never* want to be in that position again.

In late 2015, I got a call from a local hospital and they offered me the position of Director of Pharmacy. It would have been my Dream Job had they offered it to me six months earlier, but I turned it down. I had been bitten by the entrepreneurial bug. I had the fever. My business has completely changed my life.

Now, I work at home two days a week on my consulting business and only take the work that I want to do. I make a reasonable income; however, the major difference is now I actually *love* what I'm doing. I love knowing my actions are helping other pharmacists. Believe it or not, I actually wrote this book *for fun*!

I believe I can help advance the profession more through entrepreneurship than I ever could by working those twelve hour days.

This is because I am able to impact *more* patients through you! I am so excited to move my business forward by helping you succeed.

CHAPTER 2

Benefits of Being an Entrepreneur

To get you excited and motivated to start working on your business, I want to share the benefits of being an entrepreneur. Owning a business is a limitless investment, you can build a career with no salary cap.

When you own a business, you no long trade in your time (hours for dollars) and instead start building a legacy. You start building on things you are doing today, allowing your efforts to multiply and pay you dividends tomorrow. There are countless opportunities available during this time of innovation, especially in the new fields of telemedicine and telehealth.

Congratulations on recognizing this and putting yourself on the front lines of advancing the practice of pharmacy!

Lifestyle Flexibility

Owning a business provides opportunity for a more flexible lifestyle with more time freedom. For example, because of my face to face consulting business, I am location dependent because I work solely in my immediate community. However, it gives me *time freedom* because I can prepare for my cases at home. To optimize my time, I batch my patient appointments on one day a week or every other week and meet in their primary pharmacy.

If you worked as a telemedicine consultant, you could possibly achieve *location independence*. I have spoken to several ex-pat pharmacists who still wish to use their clinical knowledge to help patients and can do this from all around the world.

Working From Home

Family is very important to me and entrepreneurship has allowed me to be much more involved in my daughter's life. I work during the time that's best for me - whether that is at night, on the weekends, or even during a nap.

Working at home also takes less of a physical toll on your body. If you've ever worked in retail, you know how physically challenging it can be to stand in front of your computer all day. The 10 hour days were difficult for me. I started to have leg and back problems and gained a lot of weight. I never had time to work out or time to plan and prioritize eating correctly. My diet consisted of potato chips gobbled quickly between scripts and sugary caffeinated drinks to keep my energy levels up.

Working from home has changed all of that. Now, if I need to stop working to rest my eyes from screen fatigue, I can get on my treadmill or break for lunch at any time to make myself a healthy salad.

My new career and schedule has also allowed me to build deeper connections with family members. Now, when my aging grandmother needs to schedule a doctor's appointment, I am the first person she calls, something that would never have been possible when I was working full-time.

Job Satisfaction

In addition to limitless income potential, being an entrepreneur can actually present you with a variety of new employment opportunities. Industries love entrepreneurs because they know we are the kind of people who take initiative.

Expendable employees are happy to stay complacent; working the same jobs year after year. Even if you should choose to take another employee position, entrepreneurship can help guide you toward doing the things you love the most.

For instance, if you love talking about diabetes, niche down and specialize in diabetic education. Even focus your MTM on diabetic education. Perhaps you could create a diabetic support group or run a diabetic workshop, both examples of services that people will pay for.

Pharmacists and healthcare providers need to figure out creative ways to get paid for our clinical services and be more involved in our patient's lives. One way to accomplish this is we can get more involved in the community and offer clinical services that would support our patients.

Multiple Income Streams

Once you learn to cut out spending, balance your budget, manage debt and get a handle on your retirement planning, you can focus on *earning* more.

As a business owner, your income potential is unlimited, whereas for an employee, income potential is limited to the amount of hours they are allowed to work. Unlimited income potential is one of the most attractive benefits to entrepreneurship.

Scaling a business allows you to replicate successful systems so you can sell your product or service over and over again and provide yourself with a good source of recurring passive income.

As an employee you trade hours for dollars. As an entrepreneur, you can find ways to leverage your time for more money which helps create financial stability and builds business assets.

Tax Benefits

Disclaimer: I am not an expert on tax law; however, I have learned a few things about tax benefits. One thing that I can claim on my taxes is my home office, printing and marketing supplies, travel to pharmacy conferences, training and licensing expenses, etc.

It is something that you would have to talk with your CPA about, of course, but having a business can help you save money when it comes to tax time.

Owning a business is a great way to give you lifestyle flexibility while improving your health, interpersonal relationships, job satisfaction and finances.

CHAPTER 3

Downsides of Being an Entrepreneur

I would not be a good coach if I did not address the cons as well as the pros of entrepreneurship. Allow me to quickly share a few of the unexpected adverse effects of my journey into self-employment.

Social Isolation

Another downside that you may not realize is the lack of understanding what you do for a living. It may be difficult to identify with other pharmacists working in hospitals or retail because now you do neither. You are an independent consultant.

Many times you will be working by yourself or one-on-one with the patient so you won't have the support of a team.

It is important to have a solid support network of people surrounding you that understand your business because you won't have the support of a work community.

I sometimes miss having other pharmacists to ask questions to and bounce ideas off, but I've realized that my friends are still only a phone call away.

Self-Doubt

Everyone experiences self-doubt, also known as the imposter syndrome. One thing that previously held me back from starting my business was the feeling that I wasn't "expert enough." I didn't have any board certifications or a special residency. At first I thought I needed these things to run a successful consulting business, but I then realized that was absolutely not true, it was just me building barriers for myself.

You are likely a pharmacist too, so you are already trained in clinical services. If you feel like you need a boost of your clinical skills, I would recommend doing CE courses on the most common chronic conditions: hypertension, diabetes, cholesterol, asthma, and COPD. These are not required, of course, but only if you feel the need to give yourself a more solid confidence in your recommendations.

Owning a business is not for the faint of heart. It is challenging and can be scary when it inevitably forces you out of your comfort zone.

For me, it has been something that I was very hesitant about at first. I wasn't even sure that I wanted to put my actual name on the website! Here I am now, though, and I can honestly say that starting my consulting business has truly changed my life.

Financial Instability

Since you are no longer trading hours for dollars, your income will be less predictable and may fluctuate; therefore, you need to be prepared for that by having a solid financial foundation.

You need to become more financially responsible and realize that you're not going to have that check coming in if you don't get out there and work for it.

CHAPTER 4

Skills of the Entrepreneur

E ntrepreneurship is not for *everybody*, but it is a *calling* for many. Putting yourself out there from a marketing standpoint can be daunting, but can also be very rewarding. Marketing yourself may mean becoming a community figure; it could mean speaking at Rotary groups or educating other healthcare workers on MTM best practices or medication safety. It may mean presenting to diabetic support groups, private employers, or even in-services to hospitals or at CE programs.

Speaking is one of the best ways set yourself apart and by becoming an expert speaker; you are marketing the use of your knowledge.

One of my clients set a goal for the first quarter of the new year. He is a full-time MTM consultant pharmacist and has done more CMRs than most of us will ever do. He decided to make a goal to get on a speaker roster. Whether it is at a local district pharmacy meeting, a rotary club or even a diabetic support group, he made speaking a goal and a priority for his business.

Don't be afraid to go out and speak about your expertise. Sometimes it is easier for us to talk about our services from an educational standpoint than it is to brag about what a great job we can do.

Networking

Social media is the new pharmacy conference hallway.

I absolutely love LinkedIn for sharing ideas. For networking purposes, it is as good as attending an expensive pharmacy conference. You can meet a ton of people by sending personalized connection requests. Seal the deal by following up and saying hello to the person when they add you as a new connection.

It is a good way to share ideas, find out what other people are doing, connect with others in your industry and also receive references.

You cannot do it without a network. I encourage you to establish profiles on Twitter or LinkedIn. Follow some of your favorite pharmacists and pharmacy publications - follow the Pharmacy Times, Drug Topics - you can even follow me if you want! My Twitter is BTPharmacy and I would love to connect with you.

It does not take a long time to get a profile set up and once you do, you will be quickly impressed at the connections you are able to make.

Personal Development

A solid rapport is something to strive for, not only with your patients, but also with other providers and pharmacists.

Entrepreneurs should try to develop a well-rounded personality with many interests. This is more commonly known as personal development.

This is not to say if you are shy that you will not be as successful; however, developing a relatable, likeable personality will make things easier for you as it helps others feel more confident when referring business to you.

The best part of personal development is that it helps deepen the relationships with your patients by building loyalty. It creates word of mouth referrals. Once you develop rapport, not only will you advocate for your patient, they will begin advocating for you.

One thing that I advise is to keep a record of each MTM success story that you have. You will use these stories as ammunition when speaking to others about your program. Others want to hear about your personal experiences and how you have helped your patients. It is very important to make sure your patients are satisfied. You can accomplish this by following up with them, developing a sense of trust, and asking them for a testimonial.

It may sound overwhelming at first, but developing your own unique character will help others see that you are a person they need to know. You can accomplish this by reading business and personal development books or listening to a podcast such as *The Art of Charm* or *Entrepreneur on Fire*.

Building Systems

Another skill of the entrepreneur is the ability to create systems. Being a one-person show, you're going to work hard; in fact you may work twice as much as you would at a "9 to 5" in the beginning. You can build on the foundation you create by thinking about ways that you can create systems and put protocols in place. Systems will help free you up to focus on your sweet spot.

What is your sweet spot? It is that thing that *only you* can do. It is basically being able to offer your clinical skills and knowledge. To do that, you're going to have to train others to do the more laborious and clerical tasks for you.

As an entrepreneur, you must learn how to train others. Most of the time this is going to start with the technicians and the pharmacy support staff around you. Start by creating a protocol for identifying an MTM and offering the service in a step by step fashion. Think about the steps that you go through to look for a patient's MTM and write them down.

- Log into Mirixa.

- Go to the dashboard.

- Look through the patient information.

- Identify the patient in need of a CMR.

- Write down the patient's name, date of birth, and telephone number.

- Call that patient.

- What should they say to that patient? Etc.

Writing down everything that you do, every single step, no matter how small it seems, to explain it to someone who isn't a pharmacist, who isn't familiar with MTM is a huge step in training others to help you. If you are interested in receiving more training on how to create a system to train others how to support your MTM program you can join the e-course at PharmapreneurAcademy.com

---

Mindset of the Entrepreneur

Entrepreneurs are courageous; they try new things, sometimes fail, and then try other new things. We don't like to say "failure" in entrepreneurship, we prefer to phrase it as we have wins and we have lessons. Having a good attitude is essential to being an entrepreneur, this means having a try or die attitude. Failure is growth. Embrace and learn to love rejection, because when you get rejected, it can be a good teaching point. So have a great attitude about it. Say, "You know what? The next time I go in, I'm going to take that rejection and turn it into a positive."

For example, one of my clients said that they were having trouble finding community pharmacies that need MTM services because it's "easier" to allow their big PBM provider do it for them.

I said, "Okay. You should go in and say, 'Hey, listen. I know that you're having Cardinal/GNP/McKesson/some other PBM do these CMRs for you, but have you ever thought that maybe they don't have your best interest at heart? Whenever you see those tips that say, "change the patient to a 90 day supply", do you think they might have their own best interest in mind as opposed to the patient's?

When they change your script to a 90 day supply, they cut your reimbursement. The 90 day reimbursement is not as good as a 30 day supply; it's helping them. It's not helping your pharmacy or the patient that is already non-compliant.

This is just one example of how you can take a criticism from someone that sees MTM as a burden, turn it around, and say, "Hey, you're giving up your power here."

Another thing that entrepreneurs should have is the desire to be the "go-to "person in their industry. You want to be the person that people come to for advice, or when they see a new opportunity, you want to be positioned as the expert so that leads will come to you. You want to be known for doing MTM, don't keep that a secret. I want you to make it known to everyone that you are the expert at MTM and to come to you with any questions.

I guarantee you, by the end of this book you will know more about MTM billing, consulting and marketing than 90% of other pharmacists.

Seeing yourself as a CEO is important. You need to take your business very, very seriously. You need to invest in yourself. If you need business coaching, consult a lawyer for your LLC, call your CPA, do whatever you feel like you need to do, but don't get hung up on any one thing. Keep moving forward every day. Do not feel that you have to have a website or a business card or fancy marketing materials. You do not have to have all this "stuff" before you can get started.

I don't want it to be a barrier for you. It is icing on the cake. Your business doesn't need that stuff to be successful. If it is holding you back, leave it behind. No one will notice your lack of logo, I promise!

See yourself as the problem solver. Not only are you the CEO, but you are the problem solver. Trust yourself. Trust your instincts. Trust that there are no rules in entrepreneurship. There's nothing holding you back. If you have a workflow or a time issue, you can solve it. I want you to really take ownership of that fact. You hold the solution.

CHAPTER 5

Skills of the Business Owner

Now let's talk about how being an entrepreneur is different than owning a business and vice versa. Getting set up as a business entity may be one of the easiest parts of starting a business, but many people overthink this step. In just a few easy steps, you can be set up and ready to do business within weeks.

For me, working with a lawyer to set up my LLC was the best option. We felt the LLC gave me a little bit more liability protection than a sole proprietorship and looked more professional. Another reason that I chose the LLC is because although I don't know what the future will hold and having an LLC was my first step in taking my business seriously and putting my best foot forward.

Of course you could DIY the LLC, but as an entrepreneur you really need to start thinking about your time as being a function of return on investment. Can you do this LLC yourself? Yes. Would it take probably 8 to 10 hours if you're inexperienced in LLC formation? Probably. Do you want to focus your energy on creating the LLC, or would you rather pay a fairly nominal fee to have it handled by a professional? The same principal applies to setting up a website, etc.

For me, it's just so much easier to hand it off to a professional and let them handle it. The outsourcing of more labor intensive tasks is something that you need to learn to do. I know as pharmacists we want to keep everything close to the chest and have control, but sometimes you need to have control over your own time more than anything else.

Here is another example of when to outsource. Hiring a CPA at this point in your professional life is probably a good idea; however, when you were in school, it was easier for you to just do it on your own time using Turbo Tax. Now that you are a pharmacist, you may have a spouse and dependents and are at a point where hiring a CPA is a better return on your investment.

When you own a business, there are many new tax write-offs you may miss if you try to do it yourself through an online tax system. Knowing *when and where* to focus your time and resources is a business skill of the entrepreneur. If you plan for these upfront costs, you can be strategic in your purchases.

Just as you would enlist the help of a lawyer to file your LLC, enlisting the help of a CPA is very important in running your business because they help you take advantage of tax benefits. This is a personal choice, of course, and it could be argued against. As an entrepreneur, sometimes you need to let go of the reins and focus on your "genius". As pharmacists, most of us probably are not professionals in tax law or LLC formation.

Now that we have learned how being an entrepreneur is different than running a business, we can think about how running a business is a little bit different than being an entrepreneur. Stay with me, this does make sense.

The first steps to entrepreneurship were networking, personal development, implementing systems and having a great mindset. Now we will take a look at the first steps in business building.

First Steps in Starting a Business

Many times, the first step that you will take is to register your business in your state. Your lawyer may be able to do this for your, especially in the case of an LLC you also get a business license. This is usually a nominal fee. I believe for me, in the state of Arkansas, it was around $150.

Next you will decide which type of corporation you should use. Many times this is accomplished either through an LLC or sole-proprietorship. An S-Corp is another option, but is much more involved due to requirements for board meetings, detailed record keeping, etc.

One thing my lawyer did when we set up my LLC was ask whether or not I thought the LLC would ever own property. Of course, I have no idea whether it ever will or not. Perhaps maybe someday we will grow into a physical location, but right now I'm conducting business out of my home office. I told him to go ahead and put the stipulation in, and it was something that I really appreciated him having the foresight to ask me about.

Before setting up an LLC or a sole proprietorship, I would highly encourage you to have a consultation with a lawyer and speak to them about how much it will cost them to set it up on your behalf. For me, it was two visits, totaling a couple of hours from a lawyer that's a friend of mine. It shouldn't cost more than about $300 to set up.

In a sole proprietorship, you may not need to hire a lawyer to set up the entity. There is more information about this in the guest blog post written by my own lawyer on the BTPharmacyConsulting.com/blog.

You would have to acquire a state business license, but cost and requirements vary by state. Whether or not you're doing an LLC, I recommend that you get on your state business website and find out what the cost is to register your business. Some state boards of pharmacy require you to be licensed as a consultant pharmacist to practice in certain facilities. This usually does not apply to the community pharmacy or physician consultant pharmacist, but you should check with your state board to be sure.

Tax ID Numbers

Once you are licensed as a business in your state, the next step is getting an Employee ID Number (EIN) number. You will need the EIN number and your business license to open a bank account in your company's name.

If you do a LLC and may have people working under you, you will need what is called an EIN. The tax ID number allows you to pay your employees. Whether or not you ever plan on getting employees, you do need to have one. My bank even requires an EIN for opening a business account for a sole-proprietorship. Once your business is registered, you will need this number to set up a business account at a bank.

After you get the EIN you can open a business bank account. It is crucial that you *keep your personal and business accounts separate.*

It is very important that you keep your personal and your business banking account separate so that you don't mix funds. This may mean starting with about $500 in seed money just to pay for little things out of your business account to make it easier for your CPA during tax time.

The business license, lawyer, office supplies, etc. are all tax write-offs. It is much easier to have only one dedicated business account.

Employee vs. Independent Contractor

You and the entity will have to work out if you will be paid as an employee or as an independent contractor. Also known as the W-2 vs. W-9 employee.

There are both pros and cons to working as an employee versus an LLC or independent contractor. The difference is that you get a W-2 as an employee and a W-9, also known as a 1099, as an independent contractor.

As a W-2 employee the company holds out taxes for you. However there will be no tax withholdings for W-9 employee or "independent contractor". As an independent contractor (W-9 employee) you should plan to set aside a portion of your revenue to send in for your income taxes. I use QuickBooks Online and work with an online bookkeeper and CPA to help me plan for this expenses.

In my experience, most pharmacies are more comfortable setting you up as a W-2 employee. Just be conscientious of the differences and are comfortable with how you are being paid. Have a solid plan laid out with your CPA to cover tax liability.

Naming Your Business

When choosing your name it should be descriptive and a bit unique, but not so unique that no one can remember the name.

For example, this business is BT Pharmacy Consulting LLC. There is a great reason I chose not to use my last name, *Thielemier*, because: (1) no one can spell it; (2) no one can say it, (3) nobody can remember it. So I used BT, my initials.

Don't overthink this. Choosing a name doesn't have to be an epic production, or snazzy and over the top. It can just be your name consulting, LLC. It's not important.

More importantly, in the future you can choose a "DBA". This means *doing business as,* this is a name that can actually be changed.

For example, the name of my business is BT Pharmacy Consulting LLC. But, I can also do business as the Pharmapreneur Academy.

Like I said, don't limit yourself with anything too specific to MTM. You can include pharmacy to be more descriptive of your consulting services. However don't feel like you have to use anything other than Your Name, Consulting. Also don't limit yourself to MTM only or hospital only, etc. Make yourself memorable on an invoice, but don't reinvent the wheel.

Liability Insurance

Check your professional liability insurance to make sure that you are covered for clinical services. This is extremely important if you are going to be doing MTM services in a variety of settings. Although you may be covered by their umbrella liability insurance, you will want to have your own as well. Double check and make sure that you are going to be covered for MTM clinical services.

Personal Financial Health

I have touched on this before, but it could be an entire book of its own. Part of being an entrepreneur is that you don't have a steady income. Make sure your personal financial situation is healthy because steady financial ground is extremely important for entrepreneurs.

You can purchase health insurance on your own if you don't have a spouse to cover you on insurance. I would recommend using the HealthCare.gov website to shop for personal health insurance. It may seem more expensive because you don't have an employer contribution. When you leave your employer, you will be responsible for your own insurance coverage because, like taxes, it will no longer be held out of your check automatically.

For me, I am covered on my husband's insurance. When I first lost my job, I looked at the possibility of purchasing a plan for myself, it was about the same.

For retirement accounts, I really am a fan of Betterment. It is a robo advising fund. It is a great way that you can set up your own

IRA or investment account in a very easy to use automated investment platform.

Investing is something I'm interested in, but I realize not everybody is interested in it. Since you are not going to be able to use your company's 401(k), as an entrepreneur, you will have to look into other retirement options; Betterment is a great one. If you need a referral bonus, email me at blairthielemier@btpharmacyconsulting.com and I would be glad to send you one over.

Also, you should have a personal savings and an emergency fund set up to cover your family's expenses. The recommendation is a three to six month overhead for fixed expenses. Add up your mortgage, health insurance, and those sorts of expenses to find your monthly "fixed" or recurring expenses. If something were to happen, you need a financial cushion in order to not put your family's livelihood in danger.

Managing personal finances is a huge part of entrepreneurship and is something that you need to be thinking about now, before you leave your job and while you are building your consulting business.

CHAPTER 6

Types of Consulting Services

N ow let's discuss something exciting; getting paid for your services! We have already discussed getting paid for the implementation of new programs in a community pharmacy. Now we are going to discuss consulting service options in detail.

New Program Implementation in Community Pharmacies

For implementation of a new MTM program, you could give an estimated quote of around $3,500 for *implementation services only*. This number is based on my estimate of the hours you will spend setting up the program, training staff members and getting as many CMRs completed as you can within the agreed-upon timeline. This number is based on an approximately one-month timeline. I estimated you would be able to complete around 20 patient CMRs completed during the one-month implementation.

Ex.) Estimate 20 patients x $75 + (25-30 hours of staff training x $75) = ~$3,500

This, of course, could be changed. I don't recommend trying to implement this service in January or near the beginning of the year because every January 1st, every Medicare D beneficiary has to re-qualify for MTM eligibility. For this reason, it is going to take a while for Medicare to sort out which patients meet the minimum drug spend ($3,138 predicted drug spend per year in 2015)[1] and meet the minimum number of prescriptions and chronic conditions needed to qualify them for the MTM program. The $3,500 figure is what I would charge somebody to implement a brand new program in a pharmacy that has never done much more than look at their MTM queue.

Contracting a pharmacy with the two major MTM platforms would mean using the community pharmacy's NABP. OutcomesMTM and Mirixa are the largest platforms and the first ones to focus on when building your independent MTM consulting business. They are the easiest to use as most pharmacies are already contracted with them and will identify MTM eligible patients automatically for you.

This is the path of least resistance in setting up a consulting practice for independent community pharmacies. This is where you should start and is going to be the avenue that this book will focus on the most. There are, of course, other avenues available for consulting business. One area of promise is contracting with self-insured employers or other private payers, but for this book

---

[1] 2015 Medication Therapy Management (MTM) Submission Information [PDF]. (2014, May 7). Baltimore: Centers for Medicare and Medicaid.

we will focus on consulting for community pharmacies and physicians.

There is a sample timeline in the Pharmapreneur Academy Forum that I have created for you to go by if you are interested in doing this.

If you have a pharmacy that is not busy enough to pay you all year long and just want you to come in to train them to run the program, then you have a plan in place. Get their program set up and let them manage it the remainder of the year. This could be a good option.

This gives you an option to offer smaller-volume pharmacies that only want a program set up. You will provide them with a plan for managing their MTM program.

If you are interested, there is more information about this service in the Pharmapreneur Academy e-course.

Managing a Full Annual Program for Community Pharmacies

If the pharmacy wants you to manage the full program for the year, I recommend charging between $75 and $100 per hour for your clinical pharmacist services. This, of course, is a little bit higher than you would make as a dispensing pharmacist in order to cover the required additional training, such as an MTM certificate course or an immunization certification. You will also have additional expenses of purchasing your own healthcare coverage, retirement savings and incomes taxes (minus taxes if they choose to make you a W-2 employee). An MTM consultant is a bit more specialized and clinical specialties can expect to earn a little bit more.

For my area, $75 per hour is appropriate. I recommend that you charge a monthly "retainer fee" for managing an annual program for the pharmacy. Usually my retainer fee is a minimum of two hours a week. I have not had any complaints about this and feel confident it is a good number to start with. If the pharmacy has few MTM eligible patients or they have a lower fill volume, you may choose to lower this to a one hour per week retainer. If it is a very high-volume pharmacy, filling over 800 prescriptions per day, you probably need to charge three hours per week.

The retainer fee is a good way to manage a program and manage all the MTM-associated tasks for the pharmacy. The pharmacist-in-charge or owner won't need to worry about receiving faxes on overdue CMRs or wonder if their adherence percentages are falling because nobody is checking their TIPs. You will login in a minimum of once a week for each site and make sure all tasks are taken care of.

The pharmacies that I consult for have been relieved and happy with my services and are glad to pay me this monthly retainer fee; they know it is one less thing that they have to manage in their day-to-day workflow.

I suggest you get paid directly from the pharmacy. Again, I recommend charging $75 to $100 per hour directly to the pharmacy, with a minimum of two hours per week. You are managing their program and submitting billing on their behalf. Only a pharmacy with an NABP can contract with OutcomesMTM and Mirixa. In this direct pay model, the pharmacy will keep the OutcomesMTM and Mirixa reimbursement, effectively cancelling out a large portion of your fee.

Ex.) Say you charge for 8 hours retainer fee during the month of October (8 x $75 = $600), and billed for 2 TIPs (2 x $12) plus 2 Mirixa CMRs (2 x $75) plus 4 OutcomesMTM CMRs (4 x $60). These services would total $414 in MTM revenue. This would cancel out a large portion of your retainer fee ($600 - 414 = $186) and be easier to keep up with. I keep a record of my monthly hours with my billings and email it to the pharmacy at the end of the month.

An annual CMR would equate to around $400-500 *additional revenue* for a community pharmacy each year. This extra source of revenue is generated by several factors: follow ups, administering immunizations, increased number of refills per year (average of 3 more per year per medication), filling care gaps, OTC and front-end sales and increased customer loyalty.

So to extrapolate that if the pharmacy is paying your fee, then are still coming out on top because of the additional revenue being generated by a sustainable MTM program.

I do not recommend using a "profit sharing" model. It is difficult to keep up with and can be more trouble than it is worth. Of course if you work more than the two hour retainer on your monthly cases you would add hours to your consulting invoice and monthly timesheet. Sometimes Mirixa only gives you 21 days to complete a CMR, whereas OutcomesMTM will give you until the end of the calendar year. For this reason, there may be some months in which you will work more than two hours per week to keep your case queue updated.

Billing a monthly fee at the end of the month is the easiest way I have found to handle payment. This model will work well no matter what type of consulting you are doing; working in a physician's office, a pharmacy, accountable care organization, etc.

I don't recommend that you try to keep up with exactly what you reimburse, how you split the reimbursement, share the profits, etc. It is way too difficult to keep up with because of the lag time of actual reimbursement payouts.

This is the easiest way to deal with this issue. You only have to worry about billing the entity directly for your time or services. Someone else is handling contracts with the payers.

If you are using Outcomes and Mirixa, their platform handles the billing for you. If you are serving a physician's office, their medical coding/billing team will do it for you. I will expand on this topic more in the next chapter. Either way, the best option is to be paid directly from the entity that your are consulting for and allow them to keep all of the payer reimbursement.

CHAPTER 7

Options for Reimbursement

There are several options that you can keep in your "clinical services toolkit". The larger variety of services that you offer, the better. You never know which opportunity will contribute the most to your success, so when first starting out I recommend that you be very flexible and open to new ideas.

"Incident to" Billing in Ambulatory Care Settings

There are a few different options for reimbursement in various *ambulatory care settings* such as chronic care management services, transitions of care consulting, offering clinical coordination services in physician offices and home health agencies.

One way pharmacists can receive reimbursement for MTM services is billing with "incident to" codes. The codes start with 99211-99215. Those are usually billed in increments of numbers of minutes and complexity of the services, the least being a 15-minute incident to appointment, and the most a 40-minute incident to appointment (levels 1-5).

These are used by the medical coders in a physician's clinic to bill for MTM services. Incident to services must be offered under the direct supervision (not in the room, but on the premises) of the physician or other practitioner. Incident to services may need to be administered on a different day than the appointment with the physician if the insurance will only accept the lesser of the two bills occurring on the same day.

"Incident to" Billing in Acute Care Settings

The other types of "incident to" codes are ones used in hospitals, emergency departments and outpatient clinics. These are for *acute care settings* versus the 99211-99215 billing codes that are in ambulatory care settings. There is a hospital code, G0463, or more commonly the chronic care management code 99490 that can be used in outpatient acute care clinics.

Using Pharmacist-Specific Billing Codes

Another option would be using a pharmacist-specific billing code. These are accepted by some insurance and some Medicaid plans. You would need to test them.

For some reason, the pharmacist-specific codes don't seem to work as well as the incident to billing codes in physician's offices.

The pharmacist-specific codes are the codes you would put on the Superbill if you were trying to paper bill for MTM in a pharmacy without using a MTM platform. They can also be used to bill private insurance companies or Medicare patients who don't fit the automatic MTM eligibility criteria.

These are the codes that Outcomes and Mirixa built into their system and are using to bill Medicare. Several Medicaid programs that pay for pharmacists at specific MTM in Colorado, Maine, Iowa, Missouri, New Mexico, and the Minnesota Department of Health. These codes are 99605 through 99607.

Accountable Care Organization Consulting

Another option for reimbursement is contracting directly with ACOs or patient centered medical homes (PCMH). The value that you offer as a pharmacist is helping the physician, hospital, or home health agency decrease their costs and improve patient outcomes. In this model, you are not functioning from a revenue generation standpoint. You are functioning from a cost savings angle. You can focus on increasing their profit margins through maximizing the bundled reimbursements of a pay-for-performance model.

Accountable care organizations dealing with bundled payments are currently being scrutinized by CMS. Pharmacists can take advantage of their personal relationships with their patients and offer them *preventative care services* within ACOs or PCMHs.

For instance, the physician clinic may only get a certain amount for a patient with multiple chronic conditions. If you help cut down the time the physician needs to spend with that patient by optimizing medication regimens you can save the provider time.

By enrolling their patients in chronic care management services, conducting incident to MTMs, you can help decrease costs and improve patient outcomes.

Collaborative Practice Agreements

Another clinical pharmacy service that is gaining popularity is collaborative practice agreements (CPAs). By helping pass innovative new laws, the Board of Pharmacy in New Mexico is paving the way for more pharmacies to create CPA's with physicians.

This could be beneficial because it can help bring in more revenue for a physician's more complex patient cases (*research estimates around 15% more*)[2] and may help patients avoid costly hospital stays and ER visits.

In a collaborative practice model, you help patients avoid adverse effects due to medication intolerance and/or subtherapeutic doses. Having a collaborative practice agreement in place would allow you to immediately change therapy and reduce the risk of hospitalization due to an adverse drug event.

---

[2] Dotinga, R. (n.d.). When pharmacists partner with physicians, everybody wins. Retrieved March 10, 2016, from http://drugtopics.modernmedicine.com/drug-topics/news/when-pharmacists-partner-physicians-everybody-wins

Formal collaborative care models between pharmacists and physicians allow pharmacists to deliver clinical care services such as Medicare annual wellness exams that normally require provider status. Until pharmacists receive federally recognized provider status we much find creative ways to bill for our expertise.

Collaborative care models that include a pharmacist can help alleviate some of the demand for physician-provided care, and also can facilitate access to primary care services, especially those related to medication management.[3]

Essentially the pharmacist would perform the service, document the encounter, make recommendations, and inform the physician of any changes. This frees up the physician to see more new patients and to accept more complex patients that require extra time.

Chronic Care Management Services

As of January 1, 2015, Medicare pays for non-face-to-face care coordination services through billing CPT *code 99490. Chronic Care Management Services (CCM) may be provided by phone or telehealth by a qualified healthcare professional* [4].

Physicians' offices often pay nurses to provide Medicare wellness exams, MTM and CCM, but nurses do not always have

---

[3] Exploring Pharmacists' Role in a Changing Healthcare Environment [PDF]. (2014, May 21). Avalere Health.

[4] *Chronic Care Management Services* [PDF]. (2015, May 1). Centers for Medicare and Medicaid.

the clinical coordination skills to set up new clinical programs. Pharmacists are well suited to organizing and coordinating successful clinical programs to manage the most complex patients.

An opportunity exists for consultant pharmacists to offer CCM services in providers' offices as well. There are several companies already providing online assistance to practices for CCM services. Transitional care management and chronic care management services require general supervision (services must be under the general quality control of physicians) if provided by clinical staff.

Clinical Care Coordination Services

One opportunity is becoming a clinical care coordinator for a hospital. Or even focus on specializing in the implementation of new MTM programs amongst outpatient hospital pharmacies.

Under these models, CCM and clinical care coordinator, you would not be doing any consulting yourself or handling the MTM cases yourself. You would be coordinating and implementing the program and training others in proper management.

Transitional Care Management

Another opportunity that exists for a pharmacist who wants to consult for physician groups or work as a clinical care coordinator is the transitional care management (TCM) specialist.

Similar to the CCM services, *TCM services are billed using CPT code 99495 and 99496*[5]. These are intended to be used by a physician's clinical staff member in the 7 to 14 days post discharge from an inpatient hospital setting.

Some of the communication required can be provided non-face-to-face by a physician's clinical staff member, with a face-to-face visit scheduled within a certain window post-discharge.

It could possibly be another service that a clinical pharmacist can offer in a physician or home health setting.

Immunization Services

A vaccine clinic implementation service would be helpful and something you could offer to set up for independent pharmacies.

For instance, there is a community pharmacy in my area that goes to local private employers and provides flu vaccinations for their employees every year. They choose a day to go in and vaccinate all the employees. The employer pays them a certain fee plus the cost of the vaccines.

In a vaccine clinic implementation service you will go in and set up vaccine clinics for the pharmacy. The great part is this could be easily scalable and you could do this for several pharmacies. Your efficiency would improve and you could rinse, recycle and repeat the procedure for as many pharmacies as are interested. You could also offer it as a repeating annual service package.

---

[5] *Frequently Asked Questions: Transitional Care Management* [PDF]. (2013, February 1). American Academy of Family Physicians.

It would be a good way for independent pharmacies to market their services in the community and they would be able hire you to put the vaccine clinics together while still taking the credit.

You could also set up a travel vaccine program on-site for pharmacies that are interested in offering exotic travel immunizations such as Hep A, Yellow Fever, etc.

Depending on the state, pharmacists can administer many vaccines, but Medicare only seems to pay for the flu and Pneumovax vaccines when pharmacies are billing. I have heard physician offices say that it is actually easier for pharmacists to bill for flu and pneumonia vaccines than it is for the physician's office, so I found that to be an interesting and selling point.

Getting contracts with private businesses and employers to offer mobile or on-site immunization clinics or travel vaccine clinics could be a great business model for the new Pharmapreneur.

Diabetic Education Services

Another option and opportunity for consulting is as a diabetic educator. You could work in telehealth or an in-person setting. Some insurance companies will reimburse for this. Medicare is allowing CDE Certified nurse practitioners practice in their own clinic without the direct supervision of a physician. APNs still require a collaborative physician, but *are not required to be under their direct supervision in certain states.*[6]

A pharmacist with a CDE license could possibly join in with a clinic like this one to provide additional service offerings for their patients.

Patients may be interested in joining a diabetic support group and would self-pay for this kind of service. Again, these services can also be handled by a nurse or a dietician (and possibly more cheaply), but it is an option if diabetic education is your passion.

Find out if there is a diabetic support group in your area. If there are no diabetic educators in your area, you may be able to get referrals from physicians by creating a diabetic education program and charging patients in a cash-based model.

---

[6] Where Can Nurse Practitioners Work Without Physician Supervision? ? (2015, November 05). Retrieved March 10, 2016, from https://onlinenursing.simmons.edu/nursing-blog/nurse-practitioners-scope-of-practice-map

Pharmacogenomic Testing Representative

I have a good relationship with a pharmacogenomic (PGx) testing lab company who is committed to helping pharmacists offer PGx testing as a clinical service. If you are interested in offering genotype testing in a physician clinic or pharmacy, you can get set up as a representative for this company. I would be happy to do that for someone that is interested. The reimbursement is fair, approximately $50-100 per patient. This would be a good option to implement in your pharmacy's MTM program as well.

As a pharmacogenomic testing representative, you would help the physician setup their program, obtain the order for the test and possibly even offer to interpret the results and make recommendations on the physician's behalf.

Another option is to implement the program and train the staff, and then allow them to manage the program themselves.

The process is fairly simple: physician orders the test, patient is swabbed, sample is sent off to the lab, physician or pharmacist receives test results.

Usually the test takes three to five business days to process. You could then use the patient's results to perform a CMR or a targeted medication review (TMR) for them. In a physician's office, you would bring the patient back in to discuss the results of the DNA test. The physicians would have the opportunity to bill for this contact as an additional follow up appointment and can also utilize the "incident to" CPT code for billing. The main concern for most physicians is the lack of time associated with completing, reviewing and recommending changes based on genotype testing. As a test representative and pharmacist you could alleviate this burden for them by using your pharmacokinetic knowledge to help the physician optimize the patient's medication regimen.

If you were to offer this service in a community pharmacy, the process would be very much the same. However, in a pharmacy setting you may identify MTM-eligible patients first (using Mirixa or OutcomesMTM), then offer them the PGx test before their CMR is scheduled. This way you can use their test results during your CMR. For more information about integrating PGx and MTM services, check out my *Pharmacy Times article on the subject*[7].

Many patients are excited to know their DNA panel. It is a valuable service and a once in a lifetime test. The software created by the company I work with is extremely impressive and dynamic. I would be happy to show you a quick demo if you email me. And not to worry if your ADME skills are a little rusty, the software helps refresh any Cytochrome P450 system knowledge that may have left you since pharmacy school.

If you think you may be interested in offering this service, contact me and I will explain more about how to add PGx testing programs to your list of clinical service offerings.

---

[7] Thielemier, B. (2016, February 2). Could Preemptive Pharmacogenomic Testing Emerge as an MTM Best Practice? Retrieved March 10, 2016, from http://www.pharmacytimes.com/news/could-preemptive-pharmacogenomic-testing-emerge-as-an-mtm-best-practice

Diet and Smoking Cessation Services

Medicaid, in certain states, is paying pharmacists to provide smoking cessation counselling services. It is a small fee, but can add up.

It is something that you can keep in your bag of tricks, so to speak. If pharmacies are interested, they could hire you to do the MTM, implement a smoking cessation program and implement an immunization clinic program all at the same time.

You could offer it as part of your total consultant package.

CHAPTER 8

Identifying Your Target Market

Now that we have talked about using various "incident to" billing codes, CCM codes and various other payment options for consulting, I want you to start thinking about the opportunities discussed. Begin thinking about why you want to do consulting, the types of patients you want to see, people you want to help, the difference you want to make, and who your target market is.

Ask yourself:

- Do I want to work in a physician's office or in people's homes?

- Do I prefer working in a home-health setting or as a transitions-of-care pharmacist?

- Do I only want to work in community pharmacy?

- Is there a market for my services?

- What is the problem that I am solving?

- Are there enough people out there that would hire me?

To review, we have talked about opportunities for consulting in acute care and ambulatory care settings, providing implementation and management services in community pharmacies and outpatient hospital pharmacies, offering PGx testing, CCM services, immunization programs consultant and any kind of direct-pay model that you think will offer value to your patients.

Think of your existing skills, contacts and experience. Use these strengths to your advantage. There are so many options, so focus your effort on your desired target market first.

Focus on Leads in Your Target Market

Hopefully, you have been thinking about which leads you want to target within your desired market. After identifying your target market, only then should you begin to develop your services marketing plan. The trick is to figure out how to market your services in a way that provides more value than the cost of the service. It is the idea of *value over cost*.

For example, if you want to work with independent community pharmacies, you should create an educational program for them that will provide value. This could be in the form of in-services or group support, staff training or whatever you think they will value most.

Another great way to get your foot in the door is to offer training and implementation services or MTM workshops in your area. I have hosted and taught very successful MTM workshop programs in Arkansas. In one Saturday afternoon, you can offer a workshop for several live CE hours, make money and do a significant amount of networking with potential new clients.

One of my past clients lives in West Palm Beach; a large retirement community. She is going to senior day centers and marketing her services through providing education. She will be using a cash-paying business model to offer MTM services in these centers. This is just one of the ways she will market her services to her target market.

Develop Relationships with Leads

Rarely do you get hired on a cold call based on one single interaction. The pharmacies that have hired me are ones I have had relationships with for years. They know me or know of me. Many have had me work as a relief pharmacist in the past.

Of course, this does not have to be the case, but if you can identify potential leads that are already in your network you can start marketing to people that trust you the most.

With them, you develop and test your marketing plan, develop your educational materials and implement your pilot programs. Eventually, word of mouth gets around and other pharmacists ask your contract, "Your MTM program seems to be working really well. What are you guys doing?"

This is known as "grassroots" or referral-based marketing.

The first customer is the most important as you can develop your program and replicate it based on their experience. As with any relationship, the first step in the relationship is giving. You will help give support, provide education and be the go-to person for clinical services in your area.

Marketing to Leads in Community Pharmacies/Hospital Outpatient Pharmacies

There are community pharmacy-specific things that you should address in your educational marketing materials and in-services.

You should talk about how you help improve the Pharmacy Impact for Star ratings for Part D Plans (PDPs).

There are five weighted measures upon which community pharmacies can have a direct impact:

1. High Risk Medications

2. Adherence to antidiabetic medications

3. Adherence to antihypertensive medications

4. Adherence to antihyperlipidemic medications

5. Comprehensive Medication Review (CMR) completion rate[8]

Also reference the new 2016 measure for CMR completion rate for a five-star rating. It has to be above 76% for the plan to get that five-star rating.

---

[8] *2015MTMTrendsReport* [PDF]. (2015). OutcomesMTM.

The way the five-star rating system works is that the pharmacy provides the data to the plan, which impacts Star ratings.

The insurance plans want to contract with pharmacies that are completing their CMRs and have high EQuIPP scores. Remember the pharmacy only has an *impact* on PDP Star ratings; a pharmacy does not actually receive its own rating.

EQuIPP is a performance information management platform that makes unbiased, benchmarked performance data available to both health plans and community pharmacy organizations[9]. EQuIPP scores are used a as a pharmacy's "report card" of sorts; better-performing pharmacies help to improve the PDPs data. Direct and Indirect Remuneration (DIR) fees are also being increasingly tied to pharmacy performance measures. These are all things you should share with the leads you are marketing to.

Basically, a five-star plan is not going to want to contract with a pharmacy that is not performing well by meeting PDP goals for adherence and CMRs. The five-star plans get better reimbursement from Medicare, then the better reimbursement is passed on to the pharmacy. Improving star ratings is a great way to get in the preferred plan network and contract with higher reimbursing plans.

Another marketing/educational topic to point out is patient loyalty. Patient loyalty is enhanced when pharmacies offer clinical service programs so it should be included in your marketing strategy as well. Offering MTM programs, Med-Sync, health

---

[9] EQuIPP. (n.d.). Retrieved March 10, 2016, from
https://www.equipp.org/professional.aspx

screenings and point of care testing can improve patient retention and satisfaction.

Even by offering glucose, cholesterol, blood pressure screenings or osteoporosis screenings you can impact patient outcomes and loyalty.

Smoking cessation, immunization and diabetes education programs are all great options to talk about in your marketing and educational materials for pharmacy clinical services.

The point is patients are going to be appreciative of these additional services and you can highlight patient loyalty as a selling point for your program.

Marketing to Leads in Group Practices/Home Health Agencies

When thinking about where you can offer your services, look for group practices or home health agencies. These entities may function as ACO's and may be interested in your services in order to maximize reimbursement. In your marketing strategy, talk about ways you can save them money.

For a group home or LTC facility, explain to them how a consultant clinical pharmacist can keep patient medication costs down, improve outcomes and help decrease hospital readmissions by increasing medication safety. Pharmacists are proven to help reduce adverse drug events due to ineffective therapy or unsafe drug interactions.

You should tailor your marketing message based on who it is you are speaking to. For example, your marketing strategy in a community pharmacy would not be the same as your strategy for a group practice or a home health agency. They each require a different focus because they have differing *pain points*.

Community pharmacies care about reimbursement, insurance companies, getting in preferred networks, patient loyalty and medication synchronization programs to increase their refill percentage.

Group practices and home health agencies are working with bundled payment methods and Medicare shifting to a value-based repayment instead of fee-for-service-based repayment model. Show them how you are going to save them money, how you can help them generate more revenue and how together you can improve the quality of patient care.

This book will focus on helping community pharmacies implement MTM programs. In the e-course, I discuss how to identify workflow issues in community pharmacy and how to streamline MTM clinical interventions into your day-to-day practice while also improving star-ratings, marketing to patients and more.

CHAPTER 9

Marketing 101: Value Over Cost

B e so excited about your business that you are ready to tell every person you meet about your services. Shout it from the mountaintops of social media!

Marketing your business is a bit like dating; you would never make a marriage proposal to a new partner immediately after the first date.

Cultivating a business relationship is a lot like this. You will make your introductions, spark some interest, provide value, follow up with them and make them feel comfortable. The secret is to make them feel like you are providing more value for them than what it costs to acquire you and continue the relationship.

It is all about you having to provide more value than it costs to hire you.

Remember, *value over cost.*

Once you have provided value, your relationship will move to resemble a companionship, not unlike dating. Eventually, when you get hired, it will be like a marriage, there has to be trust, mutual respect, parallel goals and compatible personalities. They are letting you into their pharmacy and into their patients' lives. They trust you to represent them. You are a representative when you are working for them. Doing MTM, you are responsible for caring for and cultivating their reputation with patients.

Every pharmacy I work in, I treat as though it was my own store and the customers my own patients. People take notice of this. People notice work ethic. People notice when you treat their business as if it were your own. In order to take other people's businesses seriously, you need take your own consulting business seriously.

The best source of marketing is word-of-mouth referrals. In the next chapters, we will focus on developing your marketing materials so that you can get that first customer, get your foot in the door and get your business model streamlined to the point where you can replicate it and offer it to more pharmacies.

That is what building a consulting business is all about, isn't it? Replicating a successful service.

Maybe you are here because you are being called to make this your life's work and your dream career. That is exactly what we are going to focus on in the next chapters.

Developing Your Marketing Strategy

A couple of different options exist for you to begin to test and develop your marketing materials and strategy. You may be the type of person that prefers to test the waters, develop your elevator pitch and materials while testing them out in a low stress environment. Or you may be ready start cold calling leads right away. Either way, we can discuss your marketing options more in this chapter.

Putting an ad in the paper may sound archaic, but when I registered my LLC, I had several people ask me what I was doing and to congratulate me on forming the LLC. This created a chance for me to share the details of my new consulting business. I had not realized that my LLC would appear in the local paper, but putting an advertisement for your services in yours may be useful. Your consulting marketing plan will be specific to a pharmacy or a doctor's office, not directly to patients.

Unless, of course, you plan to target direct fee for service and cash paying patients; something I do not recommend when first starting out. In that case, putting an ad in the paper for something like a diabetic support group will test the market for your cash-paying services.

It is also a good idea to share about your business on social media in order to get more comfortable with talking about your "side business." It may be scary because you may think, "What if I fail? I don't really know how to explain it. What if I can't figure this out?"

Eventually you have to share about your business to gain exposure if consulting is your dream, so you might as well share it on social media and share with your friends and loved ones first.

One of the best leads I have gotten came from one of my non-pharmacist friends. My best friend, an APN at a multiple myeloma clinic at UAMS in Little Rock, was called upon by a representative of the pharmacogenomics company that I now work with. When she was talking to him about what their company did and what they offer, she thought of me because she knew that I was active in clinical pharmacy. She did not understand exactly what I was doing or what MTM is, but she knew I was consulting for pharmacies and would be interested in new ideas.

She was actually the contact that got me started learning about pharmacogenomics and it was all because she called me one day and said, "Hey, you should email this guy. I think that you would be really interested in the service that he is offering. It has something to do with medicines and DNA!" That is how it got started.

You never know where opportunity is going to come from. You need to get comfortable with talking about your business, explaining your services. Educating people on the value of pharmacists is key to your marketing strategy.

You should also call up your local college of pharmacy to share information about your business. I did this. They were very excited to hear what I was doing and actually put me in contact with another independent community pharmacy consultant. All I did was share my plans and ask one of my old professors if anyone else was doing independent MTM consulting in Arkansas. She gave me Taylor's name. I got in touch with her, now she and I have put together workshops to teach pharmacists best practices for managing MTM in their community pharmacy. In one four-CE-hour workshop we teach pharmacists about the value of MTM and how to efficiently integrate it into their workflow.

We have had a great response so far and our first workshop was a great success. We are going to see if it may be a good idea to achieve national accreditation for it in the future if there is enough interest.

I will share information about how you can also teach workshops on MTM in the Pharmapreneur Academy. It is a great way to generate income, network and provide value to other pharmacists in your area. This is something that you can replicate in your local area. I will share the information that we put together for our workshop in the Academy Forum. We called it a Community Pharmacy MTM Enhancement Workshop. It earns Arkansas pharmacists four CE hours and we offer it a few Saturdays each year. We are charging $150 per person and limiting it to 20 people per workshop. Contact me if this is something you are interested in.

This opportunity is another example of something I would have never done had I not started consulting, taken the MTM certification, let the local College know what I was building and networked with other consultants. Putting myself out there allowed me to develop opportunities and relationships that I would have never had access to before.

Here is your homework for this chapter: call your local college of pharmacy and tell them about your consulting business and ask them who you should connect with.

They may even say, "Hey, we want you to be a preceptor. We are going to send you students that are interested in clinical retail and that can help you get your business off the ground" or possibly, "We have a residency program and there are residents already doing this type of work. Why don't you go down there and shadow them for a day, and check out that model and see what they are doing?"

There are endless possibilities here. Once you start talking about your business, really owning it and being open to other people's insight. You can allow them to help you make connections because alone you really never know what opportunities exist.

It is very exciting. It is something that really changes your outlook on your career. For me, connecting with people like you and Taylor has made my job so much more exciting.

It is thrilling to not know what the future holds, but stay open to new possibilities.

Providing Value Through Education

We talked a little about in-services and educational materials, but now I want to dig a bit deeper. I posted a link in the Pharmapreneur Academy that was to the MTM slides I use for doing community programs. This will be a great start for you as they contain good statistics and information about MTM.

You are welcome to use my slides as a guide and develop your own marketing strategies based on your desired target market. Whether you decide to consult for community pharmacies, physician groups or any of the other opportunities mentioned, giving an in-service is going to depend on your market's focus and pain points.

Tailoring Your Marketing Materials to Suit Your Audience

For an in-service in a community pharmacy, I recommend using a slide presentation. A slide presentation is a good option for presenting to any large groups.

Using slides or a questionnaire would likely be the best option for facilitating support group discussions.

It is also a great way to give a presentation to the staff of a hospital pharmacy or when speaking at a local pharmacists' meeting.

One of my clients made a goal during our last personal coaching session; he decided that in 2016 he would speak at one of the pharmacist conventions in his area. He had been doing MTM consults full time for a telephonic call center for the past few years, but was ready to become an independent consultant.

He had more MTM cases under his belt than anyone I know. I told him he needed to be educating and sharing about his experiences. I encouraged him to start speaking and training other pharmacists. Right now, he is an expert on MTM and knows how it can be done better. He had never thought of it that way before; he realized that is an expert.

Depending on who and where you are presenting, alter your message without re-creating your entire program each time. You can use the statistics that were mentioned in my MTM program slides on the Forum.

If you are speaking with a physician in their office, they may want more succinct information. For a physician, I would recommend a one page flyer or an infographic (there are links to those I use in The Academy Forum) with the basics of CPT billing codes, how much revenue each one would generate, the way you could save them money and how you can help them improve patient outcomes.

I want you to get creative and incorporate your personality into your program. Include the services you can offer and include future opportunities as well. Have fun with developing these materials, because it should be more fun than work. Providing education is really is the best way to market your services.

Marketing to Cash Paying Patients

For people that are cash payers, you may want to develop a flyer to get participants to join the support group. I developed a flyer for the MTM Enhancement Workshop for free in an hour on Canva.com.

It read, "Take your MTM program to the next level," and, "Get four CE hours," and then it had "Hosted by" our names, the date, time, location and my email address so that they could email me and pre-register and get more details.

It does not have to be professional marketing materials or brochures. You can develop a simple flyer that has the pertinent information. Most importantly it should have a clear "call-to-action" so it is clear what you want the patient to do immediately with this information. Your call-to-action will probably be how to contact you.

I also encourage you to be creative and put your own spin on your fliers. Handing out flyers with a catchy title like, "Take Control of Your Diabetes," "6 Strategies for Lowering Your A1C in 2016," or, "How to Better Manage Insulin Therapy" and a clear call-to-action will help you convert more of those leads into customers.

More homework: I challenge you to do this for *free*. You can do it at Canva.com. It is a great resource. Get on Canva and find a cool template (but don't purchase any – it's a *challenge* remember!)

and you can get good ideas about how to make an infographic or a visually appealing flyer.

You can even do business cards or graphics for social media. You can develop your marketing material Canva, save it as a JPEG file to a thumb drive, take it to Staples or OfficeMax, and print it out on a high resolution printer.

Have fun with it. I want you, most importantly, not to spend any money aside from printing costs (and try to keep those reasonable). Remember, your materials are important, but not so important that you treat it as a barrier to getting started.

You should respect your marketing materials and spend some time on thinking about your goals and target market, but do not get stuck there. It is very easy to get overwhelmed and think that you need professional marketing material before you can pitch your services; however, that is not true at all. In fact, it may be your best option.

I will describe in the next chapter, the secret to using your pitch to customize your marketing materials for each customer.

CHAPTER 10

Developing Your Educational [Marketing] Materials

D eveloping educational marketing material is important. You should spend time thinking about your unique experiences and expertise.

I like to include stories about my personal experiences in my presentations. I don't like to bore people with too many statistics as they can be overwhelming and too abstract. People tend to tune out during overly statistical presentations and usually don't remember them anyway. Use stats sparingly and only to make a specific point.

Include stories because it explains both how you have helped others and how you can help *them*. It provides social proof.

One of my favorites is the story of how I got started doing MTM. It began with me taking over a program in a pharmacy where I was doing relief. The PIC hired me because he knew he was going to have to start participating in MTM. It was important to the store's future ability to get contracted with the higher reimbursing Part D Plans. He knew he had to participate in MTM in order to stay in the preferred plan networks.

This story illustrates two things: 1.) How I helped someone else 2.) Why he knew needed my services.

I want you to develop a story based on your own experiences; maybe a time when you have helped a patient or another pharmacy. Think about your strengths. Focus on what you are good at. Educate them on why they need to hire you and how you can make their life easier.

The Academy Forum exists as a place for you to ask questions and share stories. If you don't have experiences of your own yet, it is a great place to find out how other Pharmapreneurs are making a difference with their consulting businesses.

Whether you plan to consult for pharmacies, physicians, transitions of care entities or even direct pay patients, the stories that you share and your messaging can be very similar.

Giving an In-Service in a Community Pharmacy

Most technicians do not know what MTM means. They may not understand it unless they have actually seen a pharmacist do it in their store. Chances are they are not going to understand it unless you teach them. It will help them explain MTM more effectively to patients who ask about the program.

During the in-service, go over what MTM is, what recommendations you commonly make and a bit about the documentation and follow-up process. Talk about how important it is for them to get the patients to agree to the appointment and how it helps the pharmacy. Stress that the community pharmacist needs to do this because MTM is how the pharmacist funnels information from many different providers down into one cohesive message for the patient.

Think about it; a patient may have a cardiologist, a neurologist, a podiatrist, a PCP and also may see the physician's assistant or APN on occasion. They may be seeing five different providers, but they come to *your pharmacy* every single month to get their medications filled.

Remind them that the pharmacist is the single point of contact for most patients. If you think about it, the healthcare system and the providers act as a big funnel. All of the information is coming to the pharmacy through the funnel.

As the funnel gets smaller and smaller it is the pharmacist's job to make sure the information coming out at the bottom is presented in a way that the patient can understand. The pharmacist provides valuable information so the patient knows exactly what steps they need to take. They distill the information for the patient and help them set up goals. Pharmacists help improve health literacy and patient outcomes.

These are all things that you can and should talk about in your in-services: exactly what you will do for the patients, how you impact patients' lives. Stress how you will help the patients achieve their goals, lead healthier lives and manage their medications more effectively.

When you are giving an in-service, give it at the educational level of a pharmacy technician. In the Pharmapreneur Academy I discuss choosing an "MTM Lead"; to help you implement and offer your services.

Keep in in mind that some pharmacists may be unfamiliar with MTM and may need this basic education as well.

In summary, when you are providing a valuable in-service in a community pharmacy it is helpful to talk *briefly* about Star ratings and why they are important. You can talk in more detail about Star ratings to the pharmacy owner, but it is probably not of interest to pharmacy support staff members.

Staff pharmacists may not care as much about EQuIPP scores either, but owners will assuredly focus on things such as reimbursement rates, Star ratings, contracts and getting into preferred networks as they are most concerned about these types of issues.

For technicians, talk about how you are going to give them valuable new skills that can increase their value as an employee. In the PA e-course, I can teach you to train technicians to get the patient to say yes to CMRs, prepare for the appointment, integrate clinical interventions into the daily workflow process, document the CMR, how to follow up with physicians and introduce the use an organizational MTM folder system.

We will get more into detail about this later in the book, but these are a few of the things I want you to be thinking about when you are developing your marketing materials.

Try to figure out what the barriers are to offering MTM and how you can make things a bit easier for their pharmacy.

Marketing Cash-Pay Services to Patient Groups

Depending on your speaking engagement, your message is going to be slightly altered to suit the audience. The in-service you give pharmacy technicians will focus on how you create value for patients, change their lives and how MTM can help make their medications safer.

Using this same basic framework, you can shift the focus and wording to present these same ideas directly to patient groups.

When speaking with patients, one example you could offer in your explanation of MTM is how you can help caregivers manage a patient's complicated medication regimen. This would be a useful example when speaking to groups of adults who may be struggling to be the caregiver for an aging parent. Speaking at a Rotary or other civic group is a great way to get in front of these types of people.

In your presentation, explain that you won't replace their normal pharmacist, but you can act as their "adopted pharmacist" in a cash-pay MTM program. Be sure to explain how you will be more involved in their care than most community pharmacists are normally able to provide. In a cash paying model, the patients want to know you will be available one-on-one as their go-to medication expert.

CHAPTER 11

Contacting Your Leads

Now that we have talked about marketing by providing value, you can develop a marketing plan based on education and you can finally begin contacting your targeted leads!

You should have an idea of at least five leads in the market where you want to pitch your services. This is an exciting step in your new business; marketing is my absolute favorite part of building a business. It allows you to get creative and should be fun. Feel free to infuse some of your personality in your marketing.

For example, the photography on my website BTPharmacyConsulting.com and PharmapreneurAcademy.com was taken by me on my travels throughout the world.

Building a logo, building the website and building a 'brand' will come in the future. Right now, I want you to focus on using only *free* marketing tools and begin contacting your targeted leads. Your first marketing material can be a simple one-page flier or infographic to hand out during your presentation or "pitch."

Word of mouth marketing will help your business grow more than a website or logo.

Growing your business through grassroots marketing is the best kind of marketing, but in order to do that you need to get your first contract. Having a great relationship based on *value over cost* to hire you is the key to getting loyal fans.

Hopefully, you have identified your top five ideal clients because now you are going to be challenged to call them and deliver your "pitch."

"Pitching" Your Leads

When developing your pitch, think about the *one piece of information* you most need to get across. For example, it may simply be that you can raise the pharmacy's performance ratings.

The best way to develop a relationship with leads is face to face. Even if you have an existing relationship with your lead, calling and setting up a face to face appointment with them is still the preferred option.

If, during the phone conversation, you meet hesitation or resistance (due to time constraints, etc.) then it is ok to quickly pitch them your *in-service offer* over the phone. Unless specifically asked, I would not immediately mention your rates or the full service offerings at this time.

An over the phone pitch works best if you already know the lead in some way. It's respectful of them to set up a time to meet face to face as it shows that you are committed to your business. If you have no relationship with the lead, then meeting them face-to-face in your initial contact is the best option.

Either way, call the pharmacy first and find out the name of their owner or pharmacist in charge. Once you identify the decision maker, try to set up an appointment with them. Prepare a time to go in and speak to them about their needs. Talk to them more about their clinical programs and how you can help improve upon them.

Be prepared to be flexible during this discussion. You should not be reciting your pitch from memory when speaking to your lead. Instead, be conservative and ready to respond to their questions and concerns.

In summary, during your pitch:

Ask them what their biggest challenges are in regards to MTM (Lack of time? Work flow issues? Staff training?) Use their answers to further develop your pitch.

And remember that one piece of information you most want to get across? Be sure you understand what it is and make sure to communicate it effectively.

Example Pitch

This is an example of what I would say when pitch a new lead.

During the initial appointment/pitch with the pharmacist/pharmacy owner:

"Hello, my name is _____. I am an MTM consultant pharmacist and recently began helping community pharmacies improve their clinical service programs. Were you aware of the changes in Medicare Star ratings for MTM in 2016?"

They say yes or no.

You say, "CMS has introduced CMR completion rate as an official Star measure starting in 2016. Basically, this means that for an insurance plan to receive a five-star rating, its network of pharmacies needs to maintain above at minimum a 76% CMR completion rate."

They may say, "I don't understand anything about Star ratings."

You say, "Your performance scores and data directly impact the reimbursement rates of Part D Plans. The higher the Star rating for the plans, the better the plan gets reimbursed from Medicare. Therefore, higher rated Part-D plans will only want to contract with better performing pharmacies in the future."

Here they may begin to grumble about declining reimbursement/preferred networks/contracts/etc.

You say, "I know many independent pharmacies are already struggling to complete their MTM cases. Actually, the national average for the CMR completion rate is approximately 15%. I work with independent community pharmacies to bring their MTM programs up to speed and help them get the best reimbursement possible by their improving their data and giving them a leg up on retail chain pharmacies."

They are now likely wondering how you can accomplish this.

You ask,"How do you feel that your MTM program compares to the national average?"

Then they answer the question.

Now you question, "Do you feel that your staff is adequately prepared to make CMR completion rate a top priority in 2016?"

Their candid response, "Maybe."

You then say, "If not, I would be happy to schedule a time to come in and do an in-service training for your staff. We can discuss your needs and how I can help ensure you become a preferred pharmacy so you can achieve better outcomes and stay competitive in the changing pharmacy market."

It is easy enough to make a pitch. Being conversational and asking questions allows for some flexibility. It feels more natural than reading your pitch from a script. When you are engaged in this conversation keep very detailed notes on what the person says.

For instance, when you ask them the question, "How do you feel your MTM program compares to the national average?" write down verbatim what they say.

Have a pen in hand and be ready. You will use their *exact wording* to develop your marketing materials.

When you ask, "Do you feel that your staff is prepared to make CMR completion rate a top priority?"

They may say, "We just don't have time," or, "We are too small."

Or, perhaps they say, "No, because we are too busy. We are barely making our dispensing numbers as it is."

Whatever they say, take *exactly* what they say, write it down, and put their exact words in your marketing plan. These are their "pain points" (as we say in marketing) and use them to customize their marketing plan.

This way when you give the in-service you can say, "Do you feel too busy to deal with your MTM queue? Sometimes you can barely manage all of your dispensing each day as it is. How are you going to work in a comprehensive MTM program?"

See how you can turn the pain point back around? You have already identified their pain points for them and showed them how you can help.

Making MTM a priority may not be something they have thought about much before. You can use their wording to streamline your marketing plan for them and give voice to their biggest concerns.

Maybe it is that they do not have the money to hire an extra staff member or another full-time pharmacist to be able to do their clinical intervention.

Using that feedback, you say, "You don't have the staff or resources to hire another pharmacist to handle the constant flow of MTM requests. What if I could offer you two hours a week that you pay me as a consultant to come in and handle your program? Do you feel like that could be a more cost effective alternative?"

This is just one example of how you can use something they are telling you is a barrier for them and turn it around and make it a positive for yourself while addressing their biggest headaches first and foremost.

Identify their pain points and use their words to develop your marketing plan.

Tailoring Your Marketing Plan for Your Ideal Target

Now you know how to identify pain points by using your lead's own language. They may be most concerned about declining reimbursements. Now you know what to say because you can use their specific language to help them overcome barriers. Become a support system for them and let them know that you are on their team.

Try to make their lives easier, you are going to improve their patient care and in turn help them generate some extra revenue while offering their patients a valuable clinical service. You want to make it as easy as possible for them to decide to work with you.

Offer to help make their workflow more efficient. You have probably worked in many different pharmacies so you should have ideas of what will and won't work. You can help them overcome the barriers of lack of time and resources by training their staff on more workflow efficient techniques. More training on this can be found in the Pharmapreneur Academy e-course.

Be direct with their reservations and try to clear any barriers they may have.

If cost is an issue, you say, "I charge $75 or $100 an hour for two hours a week. I estimate that based on 100 CMR eligible patients I can bring in between $60 and $75 per patient CMR. Plus about $10 per TIP or education and adherence checkup. Essentially, you will break even by hiring me to run this program for you. If things change and you feel like it is not worth your while, you can cancel at any time and I will allow your staff to take over management of the program."

In fact, you may offer them a separate package for implementation services only. Help make it as easy as possible to work with you.

CHAPTER 12

Contracting with Major MTM Platforms

Them are many different MTM platforms, but for your purposes when just starting out, you should focus your efforts on the two largest platforms.

OutcomesMTM

Let's speak briefly about contracting with OutcomesMTM. There is an easy process for contracting with OutcomesMTM.com. You simply need the pharmacy's NCPDP or NABP number. Go to the website, enter the pharmacies NABP number and you will be accepted.

Usually, if the pharmacy is already contracted, they will have to accept you as an authorized user. Get login and your user information. It is a straightforward process and can all be done online.

If you need to call them, do so as a relief pharmacist. You should not be considered a "consultant" in their system. They view consultants as telephonic consultants that are off site. OutcomesMTM is focused on MTM and providing the 'face-to-face difference'.

Consider yourself a relief pharmacist because you are meeting patients face-to-face in their primary pharmacy and technically you are not a consultant.

You do not want to get blacklisted by OutcomesMTM or Mirixa because they think you are a telephonic consultant.

Off-site subcontracted consultants (aka "outsourced MTM consultants") are not looked upon favorably by these platforms. Your services are different because you are meeting patients face-to-face in their pharmacy and working with the pharmacies locally.

I have verified with both platforms that "outsourced MTM" does not apply to the local MTM consulting model.

Mirixa

Contracting with Mirixa is a bit different. You will begin the process by going to the Mirixa.com website to join. Print out the form to become an authorized user, put the user information on a separate sheet for each person you need to make an authorized user.

Fax that paper into Mirixa. Once you receive an email saying that they have your profile set up, you will have to go to the physical pharmacy location.

You must call Mirixa *from the pharmacy's landline* to get your username and password login information. This is to prevent telephonic consultants as well.

I have asked Mirixa about this before and their intention is to prevent people who cannot call from a pharmacy's landline from managing the pharmacy's MTM program.

This should not be an issue for you. The pharmacies you are working with should be in the near vicinity. I recommend doing this step during your onsite visit.

CHAPTER 13

Social Media Networking

To me, a developed social media networking platform is almost better than a website. It is entirely possibly to build a free website using Weebly or Squarespace, but it should not be the absolute first thing that you do because it *will not get any traffic without a marketing plan.*

However, if you recall, the absolute *first thing* you should do to get your business going is call your leads and provide education for others.

This way you can begin to decide what works and what doesn't. What is best for your business and what isn't.

Then, when you scale your business it will help you focus on the direction you want to go in. Maybe you will find you love doing something that you never expected.

By staying flexible in the beginning and utilizing social media accounts, you can avoid building a website right away.

Look at my own website for instance; I originally put up the website to market to people in northeast Arkansas. Turns out no one was looking at it at all, however it ended up (strange to me still) helping other pharmacists learn more about clinical services. That is the cool thing about business; you never really know where you may end up.

The moral of the story is: don't spend thousands of dollars putting up a beautiful website when you can build a nice looking one on Weebly or Squarespace for free.

If you are just absolutely itching to do *something,* put up a Facebook page and LinkedIn profile so people know how to reach you.

I absolutely recommend getting professional headshots for these accounts.

A professional photo is a must for your website, LinkedIn profile, Twitter account, Facebook page, business card, etc. It is very important that your branding is cohesive, professional and something to be proud of.

LinkedIn for Networking

More important than a Facebook page or a website, in my opinion, is a great LinkedIn page. I invite you to take a look at my LinkedIn page and connect with me.

I discourage you from making it look like a CV. Mine still does a little, but it is used strategically to show my background in community pharmacy and clinical hospital pharmacy. However, I do not include all the places I do relief, all the places I do MTM consulting, etc. because I don't think people really care about my CV.

Most people are more interested in how I can help them. I try to include a little bit of personal info about my consulting business. I use a catchy headline, "Helping Pharmacists Find New Opportunities in Clinical Retail Services" to convey that I *want* you to contact and connect with me.

Yours could be something like, "Helping Community Pharmacies Set Up Sustainable MTM Programs". Be descriptive and don't be afraid to show your personality a bit.

Your LinkedIn profile shouldn't be distracting. Remember, keep everything professional, keep everything positive, have a professional headshot, don't make it look too much like a CV and don't make it look like your personal Facebook page either.

Be sure and personalize your profile URL on LinkedIn, especially if you are using it in place of a website. It is pretty easy to do in the settings on your profile. Instead of having a long number, you can personalize it so you will have an easy to remember URL.

Mine is LinkedIn.com/in/BTPharmacyConsulting. It looks a little bit more professional so you can use it as your website if you want to connect Facebook to your LinkedIn page.

When you add new connections on LinkedIn you may see others with titles that indicate they are founder/CEO of their own consulting business or have something to do with MTM consulting in general, I encourage you to message them.

Do not be afraid to reach out to people and say, "This is what I'm doing and I see that you are in a similar field. I was wondering how your consulting business was going and if you'd like to chat about where your business is going, what you see as potential threats to the profession, opportunities you see, etc. I would be open to scheduling a short conversation at your convenience so we can chat and share some ideas."

LinkedIn is a great way to network. Last summer, I challenged myself to reach out to three new people each day for one month. That simple practice led to building relationships with people that I still maintain. Over that month, I met CEOs of companies and many other independent consultants.

It helped me get out of my bubble and realize that others in pharmacy are searching for the same things. For some reason, we feel isolated from each other, but that should not be the case. I am trying to change that with my website, my Pharmacy Times articles and Pharmacy Podcast episodes. I really do want to share ideas and everything I have learned to help others; it is the reason I wrote this book.

LinkedIn for Publishing

To help build your connections and share your ideas and expertise, I encourage you to publish posts on LinkedIn. Even if it is simply sharing what is going on in your business or the success you had with developing a client's program, these would make great "how-to" posts. Or, if you are excited about a new opportunity that Medicare is offering pharmacists, share it and add in your own insights.

Especially if you are a good writer, but even if you are not (you get better with practice), you should publish. I am available for personalized help if you need help developing your social media presence.

Publishing posts will help you stand out in front of your connections while highlighting your expertise.

When you publish a post on LinkedIn, make sure to connect it with your Facebook and Twitter feeds so you don't have to re-share it every single social media site.

Just as with a Facebook page, you can use your LinkedIn site as your temporary website until you are ready to build a business website.

LinkedIn Groups

Now that we have talked about networking and using published posts, you will learn how to use LinkedIn Groups to grow your connections and business.

One of my favorite, most active groups on LinkedIn is APhA's American Pharmacist Association group. There is another one that is just called, PHARMACISTS that is quite active, but less moderated. Another one that has wonderful MTM-related discussions is MTMS, which stands for Medication Therapy Management Services. There are also a few press and job search groups such as Pharmacy Times and Pharmacy Week that I frequent. They both put out a lot of great content. Just take a look around and see which groups you identify with.

LinkedIn groups are the best way to interact with many different people. There even some great non-pharmacy related groups about entrepreneurship and startup businesses you can join. I am even in one for self-published authors. I really enjoy connecting with like-minded people on social media.

Groups are the best way for me to connect with people, because usually people will not comment on your personal status. However, if you start discussions in these groups either asking for help or sharing information that you found, people tend to like, comment, and respond to you.

It is important when you publish posts to them in these groups as well as on Facebook and Twitter. It will help you develop connections and share your expertise and your ideas.

Direct Messaging on Social Media

I usually try to message people directly once they connect with me to say thanks for connecting and introduce myself. However, it is not considered poor etiquette not to reply instantly. If the person has a particularly interesting profile you should definitely try to reach out via direct message (DM).

I try not to send out cold, broad questions like, "Hey, I want to pick your brain, you need to give me a call!" or "What life advice would you give me so that I am successful?" just out of the blue. I get that sometimes and it is very off-putting. As when building any business relationship, don't make a marriage proposal before you say "Hi".

This is what a cold email or DM should look like, "Hi my name is Blair, I really liked this specific thing about this podcast you did or this article that you wrote. It helped me achieve this goal. Now, this is what I do and here is how we could both benefit from connecting. Are you interested in scheduling a brief call or Skype at your convenience?"

The best feedback I can get is a message (email, InMail, a Twitter direct message, etc.) saying that something I shared has helped someone else achieve some goal. Try to be as specific as possible with your feedback, it will open more doors.

I challenge you to make three new connections each day for a month and see what happens. If the person is someone you would like to develop a relationship with, do not be afraid to send a custom connection request by saying, "Hi, your profile is interesting. I would love to learn more about your business. Would you care to connect with me?" Then reach out to them when they accept your connection request and follow up.

Another challenge is to get to 500+ connections on LinkedIn. Don't be afraid to connect with people you don't know personally. Remember, the more connections you make, the more opportunities that will potentially come your way.

I am a big believer in social media networking and reaching out to share new opportunities and ideas with others. It is really the best way to quickly grow your network.

Using Twitter for #Pharmacy

Setting up a Twitter account is quite simple; however, the platform can be overwhelming. On Twitter, people use hashtags (#) to make a word searchable. It is similar to using a keyword search in Google. Think of Twitter like a Google search bar where you will be using hashtags as your keyword search. Whenever you post tweets use #communitypharmacy or #MTM or #clinicalpharmacist to help people find you.

For instance, I use the #personalfinance hashtag to tag articles I have written about pharmacist personal finance. Due to this, I have gotten followed by a lot of personal finance professionals and have had them share or retweet my tweets.

You can also create "lists" on Twitter to *politely stalk* your influencers. Create a focused list so you can narrow in on who you really want to create a relationship with. You will be able to look at your specific list and not hundreds of other tweets that can be distracting. Using lists, you can closely follow certain people, find out what they are interested in, find some common ground and make a connection with those people. You can also follow trending topics on Twitter, similar to an instant newspaper headline.

If I like a blog or a podcast, I will find them on Twitter, subscribe to their blog, listen to their podcast and join their community. After I have done a little reconnaissance work on them to make sure they would be a good fit for my business, I might reach out to them personally and say, "Hey, I like what you are doing!"

This is actually how I met the Pharmacy Podcast producer. Todd and I actually followed each other on Twitter for a long time before we ever spoke. I think we were both keeping an eye on one another from afar. Finally he messaged me and said, "I think you would be a really good fit for the show." And by then I was like, "Sure, I have been listening to the show for months now, just waiting for somebody to ask!"

One of the great things about Twitter is you never know who is managing the Twitter account. Twitter is actually how I met and formed a relationship with my contact at Mirixa. Admittedly, Twitter can be frustrating when you first start using it, but don't give up because it can be really helpful. You never know who is on the other side of that social media account. I personally have had two big opportunities now that have come solely from Twitter.

CHAPTER 14

Final Thoughts

In the final chapter, I want to talk about how to add to your consulting services by testing new services and acting quickly on potential opportunities.

Remember, always follow up on new leads, once you have gotten the first pharmacy under control and have systems in place, you can replicate your service offerings.

I want you to continue growing your business. That means following up on new leads, asking them to refer you to other pharmacies that need your help and focus on growing and scaling your consulting business. The idea is to build a business that will eventually produce a full-time income.

Stay flexible with your program; not every pharmacy or physician's office you work with will have the same needs. You need to be flexible and willing to accommodate them. Listen to their staff and listen to their ideas on what works best for them.

I also encourage you to continue your pharmacy business education by joining some mailing lists: the APhA, the Pharmacist's Letter, OutcomesMTM and Mirixa newsletters, the

Pharmacy Podcast Show, Pharmacy Times, and of course my Pharmapreneur Community newsletter are all great resources.

That is your homework for the final chapter of this book; take a pledge to continue your MTM education and pay it forward by educating others. As always, if you have any questions please feel free to reach out to me at BTPharmacyConsulting.com

Treat Yourself as CEO

Practice introducing yourself as the founder of your company and using your company name. It is part of taking your business seriously. This is not a hobby. This is your business which means you cannot do too many things for free. You are not going to offer discounted rates for friends because you know that your service is more *valuable than the cost to acquire you.*

If people want to work with you they will. Don't discount yourself because if people are asking you for discounts they are probably not your ideal target anyway. You want to try to work with people who are excited to work with you.

- Value your time.

- Be the one to find solutions.

- Be confident in yourself.

- Over-deliver to your clients.

- Constantly seek new opportunities for growth.

MVP = Minimum Viable Product

Every time you get your business debit card out, I want you think about minimum viable product (MVP). Act first and spend last. Avoid spending money if possible. If you do have to spend it, try to get it on a payment plan help maintain cash flow.

Also, always do your due diligence. If someone is saying that you need to sign up for this software, don't take their word for it! If someone wants you to pay a monthly fee, be wary. The more money that you put into this business the more patients and the more people that you are going to have to sign up to make it sustainable.

Always consider your ROI. If you *absolutely must have* this software to do your first patient, ask for a free trial. Then research like mad to find out if you could use another free service instead.

This is why I say the path of least resistance is using the OutcomesMTM and Mirixa platforms. Or even just using the physician's existing electronic medical record instead of spending money up front on software. The same applies to marketing and building a website, remember?

Really think about what is the least it would take to get your product to market. This is the minimum viable product cost. Once you have your business up and running and are profitable in revenue, then you can look for other ways to streamline your business - hire people, do marketing campaigns and that sort of thing. Now is *not the time* for that.

Right now, only think about your business as a business. Do not spend a lot of money on the front end. Develop a product (your MVP) and start selling that product. Only then, if you make a little bit of money on it, should you reinvest it into the business.

Big Mistakes I Have Made

Of course I have made some big mistakes! This is the reason I literally "wrote the book" on this subject!

I am not perfect. I do not have it all figured it out.

As the landscape of pharmacy changes, opportunities for clinical pharmacy will change. I already suspect we will have to adapt our business model again. Don't fall into the trap of complacency when you find some success or you will be behind the innovation curve once again. On the other hand, we don't need to just give up if the road seems difficult. Entrepreneurship is not easy.

The biggest problem I have is saying "yes" too often. Realize if you are saying "yes" to one opportunity, it means you will have to say "no" to another in the future.

Think about guarding your time as a function of ROI and MVP. Your time is one of your most valuable resources. It is the only non-renewable resource we have control over.

I am also guilty of buying business cards, building a website and marketing my business before I knew what exactly I wanted to do. Yes, this is filed under the Big Mistakes!

I went overboard with this and wasn't flexible; the opposite of the ideas of MVP and staying adaptable. Please don't make the same mistake by spending money on silly business cards, a logo, marketing materials and a website *before you ever have your first client.*

Honestly, I have had my business cards for probably about two years and I don't think I have handed out more than five. Nobody cares about business cards. Nobody.

But...if you want to go ahead and do business cards don't let me stop you. Just make sure to use a *professional picture.*

With the business card, it may be helpful if you plan to do speaking engagements so people can follow-up with you.

In summary, if you do a business card make sure you have got your email address on it. Make sure that you use it to connect with other people and get their email addresses especially at networking events. Just collecting business cards is useless unless you have a follow up plan. Don't kid yourself into thinking because you have a ton of cards it will translate into tons of leads.

The only idea is to use those cards to get email contacts for leads *that are interested in your services and interested in working with you.*

MOO.com has some really nice-looking business cards if you decide you must, but they are more on the expensive side.

I am not totally against business cards; in the future they are a great tool. I am merely against getting them before you get your business off the ground and you are ready to expand.

Certifications for MTM and ROI

What certifications do you need to do MTM? Certifications just to begin building your business are absolutely *not required.*

The APhA certification course was not as helpful as I had hoped from a business standpoint, which is the reason I created the "How to Build an Independent MTM Consulting Business" E-course, a good, broad depiction of what MTM is and why it is important. It did not give me the information that I wanted like proper billing techniques, troubleshooting and best practices for following-up with doctors.

Do you need an immunization certification? No, but you may need it to administer vaccines during the CMR.

Do you need an MTM certification? No, but it could be helpful if you want to become an expert in the field.

Do you need a board certification? Absolutely not. If you want to get it in the future to improve your clinical skills, then more power to you.

When looking at certification options for MTM, as a business owner you should think about every dollar you spend in regards to return on investment (ROI). It is easy to think, "I need a master's degree or I need a board certification," but that is really only you making more barriers to starting your business.

Unless you are *already* working a contract that *requires* you have an advanced certification, most people will not care either way if you have a master or board certification. If anything, you could do board certification in ambulatory or even geriatric care to beef up your clinical skills.

Should you decide to seek board certification, even though I don't particularly recommend it if you are focused on owning a business, there are several good training websites for board cert preparation.

A friend of mine owns MedEd101.com. He has some great resources to help prepare you for the ambulatory care, the geriatric and the consultant pharmacist board certification tests. I definitely recommend his website if you are interested in getting certified.

As for me, there is not enough ROI on my time for seeking higher level certifications at this time. Your business will not do better because you have a master's degree or a board certification. Unless you want to move into a management position at an institution or company, you *will not get enough ROI on your time and money for these certifications.*

I do recommend doing the APhA MTM certification course so you can learn how to teach your own MTM workshop! It is a bit expensive, but it may be worth it to highlight your expertise in MTM.

In conclusion, don't feel like high level certification is the next step. If anything, it is only a confidence booster and it will only delay you starting the business of your dreams. If you absolutely must, the next step should be getting an MTM Certification through APhA and even this is not an absolute requirement.

Over-deliver to Your Clients

Rule #1 in business is to excel at your work and be easy to work with. Over-delivering to your clients is something we as pharmacists tend to do anyway.

We not only fill prescriptions quickly and correctly, we also make sure the insurance is correct, look for ways to save the patient money and help them to overcome barriers to adherence, etc. We do all of these things that people don't realize we do for them for no extra payment.

In the future, we need to share about the work it takes to fill an Rx and how much trouble we are actually going through for our patients.

As a profession we are working towards provider status, but for now having a "can-do" attitude and staying positive makes a huge difference.

We all know reimbursement is a constant struggle. We know that DIR fees and PBMs are cutting into pharmacy profits. However, there are always other ways for a pharmacy to generate revenue. There are plenty of pharmacies out there doing well. I know that MTM reimbursement rates aren't where we want them to be. However, I do feel there is enough room in there that we can make it sustainable for a pharmacy or physician's office to use our services. So focus on your dreams and stay positive.

New Opportunities

One opportunity that is starting to gain momentum is the trend of hiring pharmacists to be involved in an accountable care organization (ACO)[10]. Pharmacists can help entities who have capitated fees based per patient. We can help them save money and improve outcomes.

---

[10] *Developing Trends in Delivery and Reimbursement of Pharmacist Services* [PDF]. (2015, November 1). Avalere Health LLC.

It is a viable and valuable service. Continue to look outside of the box for the value we can offer to other healthcare providers and to our patients.

Also, I want you to become the MTM guru in your area and help educate others. This is the "ripple effect" I hope to create through this book. Please "pay it forward".

I want to congratulate you as well!

Reading this book was a huge first step towards creating your Dream Career. I hope that you feel like you learned enough about MTM, Star ratings, and pharmacy consulting that you feel comfortable continuing your education and sharing your knowledge with others.

I hope that you will spread the knowledge that you have learned here. Don't keep this knowledge to yourself; please share it.

I am a big believer in having an abundance mindset. A scarcity mindset is limiting, while an abundant mindset is freeing. Scarcity mindsets will make people think, "If I tell them how I was successful, then there won't be *enough left for me*".

Having a scarcity mindset and safeguarding information is what has gotten our profession into trouble in the past. The slow decline of independent community pharmacy, the rise of huge retail chains...

Sharing new opportunities, what is working for you and how to optimize clinical services may help us save ourselves.

Information is a valuable asset that we should be sharing. As successful consultants, we need to lift each other up. Ever heard the phrase, "A rising tide raises all ships"? I truly believe in this and it is the reason I share this information so freely with you.

Have Confidence

Sometimes saying "yes" then figuring out how to do something is a better option than getting everything all figured out before you can begin.

For example, a physician's office wants you to make MTM recommendations on homeopathic supplements and natural remedies. Say yes; *then figure out how to do it.* If that is what they want, you have the training to teach yourself anything you could possibly want to learn.

People hold themselves back with excuses. Excuses like Medicare compliance issues, HIPAA encryption issues, liability issues, marketing logos, websites, lawyer contracts, etc. There will be many questions in your journey.

There are always answers. You are the solution finder. The technology is out there to can help you manage all these issues and more. You just have to get started and *find the solution* as you go.

Please, don't get tripped by thinking that you need to have everything figured out before you ever start.

Sometimes, by testing the market is the best option when we are forging a new path. Say yes, then figure it out as you go; it is the way of the entrepreneur, the solution finder.

Value Your Time

Rule #2 in business: Value your time and don't waste other people's time.

This may even mean saying "no" which is difficult for me too. When you become successful there will be people reaching out to you and asking for input on certain software platforms, different MTM programs, proprietary products and all kinds of things.

As you become more and more successful, people are going to require more and more of your time and ask for your advice.

The hardest thing for me is when I get an email that says "I'd like to chat with you". They don't mention who they are, why they are asking for my time, what it is about or why they want to chat. It makes me not even want to respond because I feel like they are already wasting my time. I feel they are trying to reel me in with a (vague, but promising opportunity!) to get me on a phone call.

Once you get into business you realize how valuable your time is and how valuable other people's time is as well. This one of my biggest pet peeves and the one that I struggle with the most because I genuinely want to help.

Even if it is from a well-meaning person needing advice, if they aren't specifying what exactly it is they want from me and why it is a waste of my time.

You will likely have similar issues because you will be seen as an expert in your field.

Continue to Grow

Stay on a personal development track. I am a big believer in personal development. I try to read ten pages of a personal development book every day.

Most of my favorite books are business books. One of my favorites is the *Slight Edge* by Jeff Olson. Malcolm Gladwell has a book called *Outliers* and that is a really book as well. There are several others that I could recommend, if you are interested please email me.

I also love to listen to business and personal growth podcasts; anything that deals with personal growth, positivity, mindset and productivity.

Because as John Rohn so eloquently put it, *"You are the average of the five people you spend the most time with."*

For me, being somewhat geographically isolated, it is hard to find like-minded people that are traveling on the same path as me. I count the podcast hosts and guests as people that I spend a lot of time with. I am constantly listening to their advice and mentorship so I count them as "my people".

I also have a wonderful business coach Natalie and mastermind group of women entrepreneurs that helps me with my personal and business development. This has been no less than life-changing for me. The PharmapreneurAcademy.com and this book would not exist without them pushing me to do it!

Try to educate yourself every day. Whether it is listening to one new podcast a day or reading ten pages of a business book each day make personal development a goal.

Also realize that failure is merely a lesson. Learn from it; be very flexible. Failing once is not the same as failure.

I sincerely hope that you will find joy and happiness in your Dream Career.

Conclusion

opefully this book has given you the knowledge and the confidence to move forward with building the consulting business of your dreams.

If you enjoyed this book, the greatest compliment you could give me is a review and to refer a colleague to my work. I sincerely hope that you will stay in contact and let me know how this information has influenced your practice.

Thanks so much for reading, I hope to continue this conversation and see you in the Pharmapreneur Academy! - Blair

Your Action Steps:

1. Decide on a business entity structure (LLC/sole proprietor/S-Corp)

2. Decide on a target market

3. Make a list of your ideal leads

4. Begin to contact your leads

5. Develop your educational marketing materials (Give Value)

6. Pitch your services in your presentation (The Ask)

7. Follow up until you get a "yes"

8. Systematize your services

9. Ask for referrals

10. Replicate and grow your business

Made in the USA
Columbia, SC
28 May 2020

98435054R00065